# UTAH

**Sarah Tieck**

Big Buddy BOOKS
Explore the
United States

## VISIT US AT
### www.abdopublishing.com

Published by ABDO Publishing Company, PO Box 398166, Minneapolis, MN 55439.

Printed in the United States of America, North Mankato, Minnesota.
052012
092012

 PRINTED ON RECYCLED PAPER

Coordinating Series Editor: Rochelle Baltzer
Contributing Editors: Megan M. Gunderson, BreAnn Rumsch, Marcia Zappa
Graphic Design: Adam Craven
Cover Photograph: *Shutterstock*: Logan Carter.
Interior Photographs/Illustrations: *Alamy*: Douglas Pulsipher (p. 9); *AP Photo*: North Wind Picture Archives via AP Images (p. 13), Douglas C. Pizac (p. 21), The Canadian Press, Chris Young (p. 25); *Getty Images*: GEORGE FREY/AFP (p. 26), Photo Researchers (p. 23), Ed Reschke/Photolibrary (p. 30); *Glow Images*: Arco Images GmbH Diez, O. (p. 30); *iStockphoto*: ©iStockphoto.com/GomezDavid (p. 30), ©iStockphoto.com/LUGO (p. 11), *Shutterstock*: John Blanton (p. 26), Darren J. Bradley (p. 27), Bryan Brazil (p. 29), Eric Broder Van Dyke (p. 5), dibrova (p. 17), Alexander Gordeyev (p. 27), Aron Hsiao (p. 11), Philip Lange (p. 30), Lee Prince (p. 19), Jerry Susoeff (p. 27), Andy Z. (p. 9).

All population figures taken from the 2010 US census.

### Library of Congress Cataloging-in-Publication Data

Tieck, Sarah, 1976-
  Utah / Sarah Tieck.
    p. cm. -- (Explore the United States)
  ISBN 978-1-61783-383-0
  1. Utah--Juvenile literature.  I. Title.
  F826.3.T47 2013
  979.2--dc23
                              2012017232

# Contents

# ONE NATION

The United States is a **diverse** country. It has farmland, cities, coasts, and mountains. Its people come from many different backgrounds. And, its history covers more than 200 years.

Today the country includes 50 states. Utah is one of these states. Let's learn more about Utah and its story!

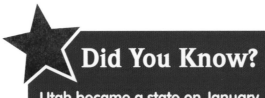

**Did You Know?**

Utah became a state on January 4, 1896. It was the forty-fifth state to join the nation.

The Great Salt Lake is one of the country's largest natural lakes. It is saltier than the oceans!

5

# UTAH UP CLOSE

The United States has four main **regions**. Utah is in the West.

Utah has five states on its borders. Idaho is north and Wyoming is northeast. Colorado is east. Arizona is south. Nevada is west.

Utah has a total area of 84,897 square miles (219,882 sq km). About 2.8 million people live there.

# REGIONS OF THE UNITED STATES

= West
= Midwest
= South
= Northeast

CANADA

WASHINGTON
MONTANA
NORTH DAKOTA
MINNESOTA
VERMONT
MAINE
NEW HAMPSHIRE
MASSACHUSETTS
OREGON
IDAHO
WYOMING
SOUTH DAKOTA
WISCONSIN
MICHIGAN
NEW YORK
RHODE ISLAND
CONNECTICUT
IOWA
PENNSYLVANIA
NEW JERSEY
NEBRASKA
ILLINOIS
INDIANA
OHIO
Washington DC ★
DELAWARE
MARYLAND
NEVADA
UTAH
COLORADO
KANSAS
MISSOURI
WEST
VIRGINIA
VIRGINIA
PACIFIC
OCEAN
CALIFORNIA
KENTUCKY
NORTH CAROLINA
ATLANTIC
OCEAN
TENNESSEE
SOUTH
CAROLINA
ARIZONA
NEW MEXICO
OKLAHOMA
ARKANSAS
MISSISSIPPI
GEORGIA
TEXAS
LOUISIANA
ALABAMA
FLORIDA
GULF OF MEXICO
ALASKA
MEXICO
HAWAII
PUERTO RICO

N
W E
S

7

# IMPORTANT CITIES

Salt Lake City is Utah's **capital**. It is also the state's largest city, with 186,440 people. This city is located near the Great Salt Lake. It is home to many businesses. It is also the base of the **Mormon** church. A famous building called the Mormon Tabernacle is in the city.

### Did You Know?

There is a monument honoring seagulls in Salt Lake City. It was built to honor the birds that once saved the area's crops.

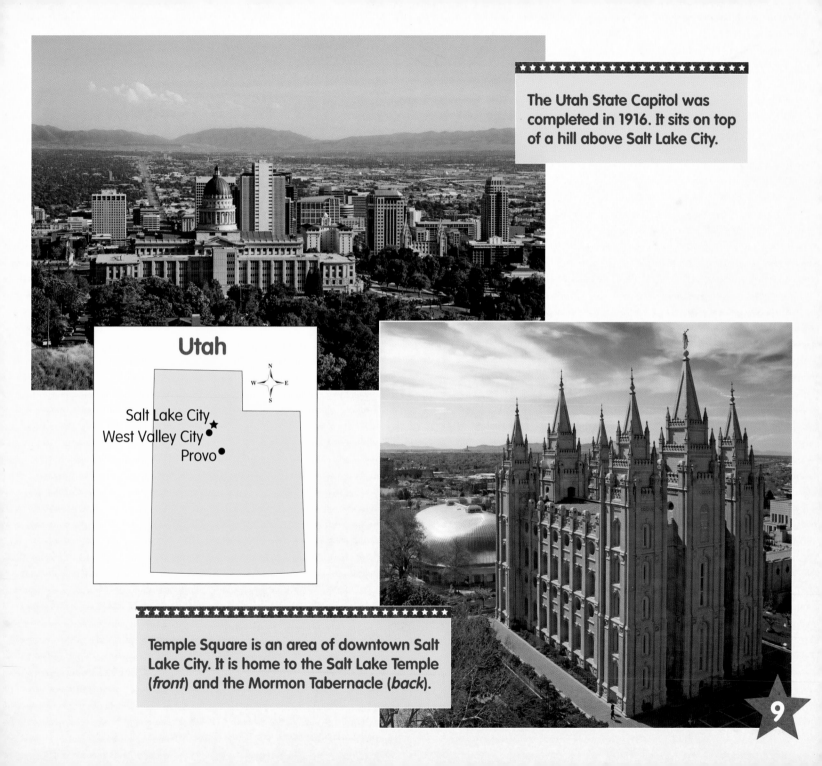

The Utah State Capitol was completed in 1916. It sits on top of a hill above Salt Lake City.

## Utah

Salt Lake City
West Valley City
Provo

Temple Square is an area of downtown Salt Lake City. It is home to the Salt Lake Temple (*front*) and the Mormon Tabernacle (*back*).

9

West Valley City is Utah's second-largest city. It is home to 129,480 people. It is part of the Salt Lake City **metropolitan** area. In 2002, the men's and women's Olympic hockey games were played there.

Provo is the state's third-largest city, with 112,488 people. Brigham Young University is located there.

The Oquirrh (OH-kuhr) Mountains are west of West Valley City. The Jordan River forms the city's eastern border.

Provo is in the Utah Valley. The Wasatch Mountains are near the city.

11

# Utah in History

Utah's history includes Native Americans, explorers, and settlers. Spanish explorers arrived in what is now Utah in 1765. They met Native Americans, who had lived there for thousands of years. In the late 1840s, **Mormons** began to settle in the area. They came seeking **religious freedom**.

The Utah area belonged to Mexico until 1848. In 1850, the Utah Territory was established. Its people wanted it to become a state. But, the US Congress disagreed with some of the Mormon beliefs. So, Utah didn't become a state until 1896.

The Mormons had a long, hard journey from Illinois to Salt Lake City. They carried their belongings in wagons and carts.

# Timeline

**1824**

Jim Bridger was one of the first white people to see the Great Salt Lake. He tasted the salty water and thought it was an ocean!

**1850**

The Utah Territory was created. Young became its governor.

**1896**

Utah became the forty-fifth state.

1800s

Brigham Young and a group of **Mormons** arrived in what is now Utah. They founded Salt Lake City.

The United States gained the Utah area from Mexico.

**1848**

**1847**

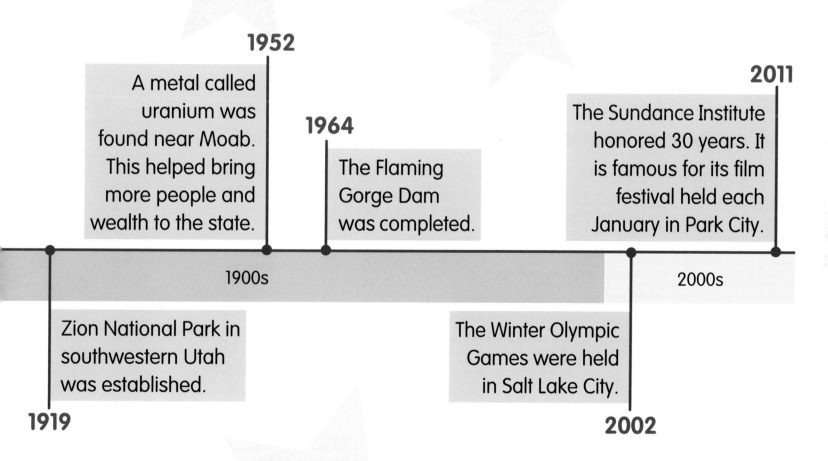

**1952**

A metal called uranium was found near Moab. This helped bring more people and wealth to the state.

**1964**

The Flaming Gorge Dam was completed.

**2011**

The Sundance Institute honored 30 years. It is famous for its film festival held each January in Park City.

1900s

2000s

Zion National Park in southwestern Utah was established.

The Winter Olympic Games were held in Salt Lake City.

**1919**

**2002**

# ACROSS THE LAND

Utah has deserts, mountains, rivers, and **canyons**. Major rivers include the Colorado and the Green. The Rocky Mountains and the Great Salt Lake Desert are also part of the state. Bryce Canyon and Zion are two of Utah's national parks.

Many types of animals make their homes in Utah. These include badgers, skunks, trout, and snakes.

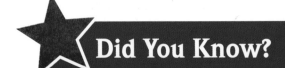

**Did You Know?**

In July, the average temperature in Utah is 73°F (23°C). In January, it is 25°F (-4°C).

Bryce Canyon National Park is known for its unusual rock shapes.
It is also known for the reds and oranges that color the rock.

# Earning a Living

Utah has many important businesses. Some people work in service jobs, such as helping visitors. Others work in construction. And, companies in Utah make **electronics**, computers, and spacecraft parts.

Utah has many natural **resources**. Its mines produce coal, natural gas, oil, and copper. Utah's farms produce beef cattle and milk. Hay is the leading crop. But, most of the state's soil is not good for farming.

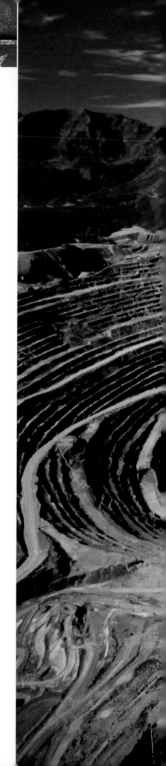

The Kennecott Bingham Canyon Mine is an open-pit copper mine. More copper has come from this mine than from any other in the world!

# SPORTS PAGE

Utah is home to many sports teams. These include the Utah Jazz basketball team and the Real Salt Lake soccer team. Utah colleges are known for strong basketball and football teams.

Utah hosts sporting events as well. In 2002, Salt Lake City hosted the Winter Olympic Games. And, Bonneville holds auto races at the Bonneville Speedway.

The University of Utah and Brigham Young University football teams are rivals. Fans get excited to see them play each other!

21

# HOMETOWN HEROES

Many famous people have lived in Utah. Brigham Young was born in Vermont in 1801. He moved to Utah in the 1840s so he could practice his religion freely. He established the base of the **Mormon** church there.

In 1850, Young became the first governor of the Utah Territory. He encouraged people to move to Utah. And, he helped build Salt Lake City and other towns.

**Did You Know?**

Brigham Young University in Provo is named for Young.

Young led the Mormon church and founded Salt Lake City.

Donny Osmond was born in Ogden in 1957. He became a famous singer in the 1960s and 1970s. He and his sister Marie starred in the *Donny and Marie* television show from 1976 to 1979.

Later, Osmond performed in **musicals**. In the 1990s, he was in *Joseph and the Amazing Technicolor Dreamcoat*.

In 2009, Osmond appeared on *Dancing With the Stars*. He and his partner won!

Osmond and his sister still perform live shows together.

# Tour Book

Do you want to go to Utah? If you visit the state, here are some places to go and things to do!

 ★ **Swim**

Float in the Great Salt Lake! The salt in this large lake makes it easy to stay afloat.

 ★ **Cheer**

See an auto race at Bonneville Salt Flats. The flat salt beds are hard, like cement!

 ## ⭐ Play

Hit the slopes in the mountains of Utah. People also hike, bike, and camp on Utah's land.

## ⭐ Remember

See the Golden Spike National Historic Site. This honors the 1869 completion of the first railroad to cross the United States.

## ⭐ Discover

See thousands of red rocks shaped like arches at Arches National Park. Landscape Arch measures 306 feet (93 m) across!

# A GREAT STATE

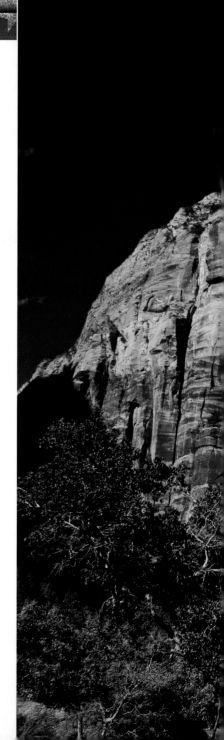

The story of Utah is important to the United States. The people and places that make up this state offer something special to the country. Together with all the states, Utah helps make the United States great.

Zion National Park is known for its red cliffs and desert landscape. People enjoy hiking and camping there.

# Fast Facts

**Date of Statehood:**
January 4, 1896

**Population (rank):**
2,763,885
(34th most-populated state)

**Total Area (rank):**
84,897 square miles
(13th largest state)

**Motto:**
Industry

**Nickname:**
Beehive State

**State Capital:**
Salt Lake City

**Flag:**

**Flower:** Sego Lily

**Postal Abbreviation:**
UT

**Tree:** Blue Spruce

**Bird:** California Seagull

# Important Words

**canyon** a long, narrow valley between two cliffs.

**capital** a city where government leaders meet.

**diverse** made up of things that are different from each other.

**electronics** products that work by controlling the flow of electricity. These often do useful things.

**metropolitan** of or relating to a large city, usually with nearby smaller cities called suburbs.

**Mormon** a member of a religious group started by Joseph Smith in 1830 in Fayette, New York.

**musical** a story told with music.

**region** a large part of a country that is different from other parts.

**religious freedom** the freedom to pray and worship as one chooses.

**resource** a supply of something useful or valued.

# Web Sites

To learn more about Utah, visit ABDO Publishing Company online. Web sites about Utah are featured on our Book Links page. These links are routinely monitored and updated to provide the most current information available.

**www.abdopublishing.com**

31

# Index